Introduction

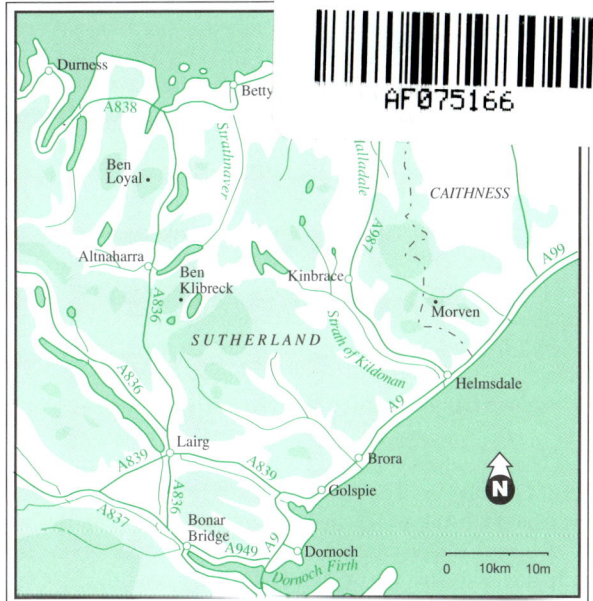

This guide is dedicated to the eastern half of Sutherland: that vast tract of wild land, named the 'South Land' by early Viking settlers, that covers much of the far north of Scotland.

'East Sutherland', as set out by this guide, includes an area defined in the east by the boundary with Caithness and the North Sea coast from Helmsdale to Dornoch. The Dornoch Firth and Strath Oykel form the southern boundary. An arbitrary line from a point about half way up Strath Oykel in the south to Tongue in the north forms the western boundary. To the north is the treacherous Atlantic coast.

East Sutherland is an area of considerable natural beauty, and though it largely lacks the dramatic mountainous scenery of the west of Sutherland (see *Walks West Sutherland*) it has its own attractions. A wide variety of coastal, forest and moorland scenery awaits the visitor, and such mountains as there are, being more isolated, offer unrivalled views.

Access to the area from the south is easy and direct, thanks to the A9 trunk road. The main road north from Inverness used to wind westwards to avoid the Beauly, Cromarty and Dornoch Firths, passing through Beauly, Muir of Ord, Dingwall and Bonar Bridge on the way. Nowadays, thanks to a trio of bridges over the firths, the road cuts straight across the Black Isle and Easter Ross before continuing up the east coast of Sutherland. Inland, the village of Lairg has good road links, but outwith these roads travel is at a slower pace along single-track 'main' roads – beautiful, as long as you are not in a hurry! The coast roads are busier than they once were, due to the popularity of the 'North Coast 500' touring route.

The area also boasts good rail links from Inverness, as the Far North rail line (linking Inverness with Thurso and Wick) takes great loops inland to Lairg and Strath Halladale. The Brora to Golspie walk (*25*) uses the railway to facilitate a point-to-point walk.

Most of the region's population is now scattered around the coastal villages of the north and east, the small village of Lairg being the largest inland settlement. The remainder of the area comprises some of the most sparsely-populated land in Europe. This is due in part to the Highland Clearances of the 18th and 19th centuries, which had a devastating effect on the population. More information on the Clearances can be found at the Strathnaver Museum at Bettyhill (*4*).

The walks in this guide have been carefully selected to cater for a wide range of ability, and to encompass most types of landscape typical of East Sutherland. A mixture of coastal, moorland, mountain and forest walks have been included.

There are few high peaks in the area, but the region's main mountains are explored in routes up Ben Klibreck (*7*), and Ben Loyal (*6*), while the prominent

Ben Loyal (see Walk 6)

Walks East Sutherland

walk	grade
1 Melvich Bay	B
2 Strathy Point	B
3 Armadale to Poulouriscaig	B
4 Around Bettyhill	B
5 Invernaver Nature Reserve & Broch	B
6 Ben Loyal	A+
7 Ben Klibreck	A+
8 Loch Badanloch & Creag an Alltan Fheàrna	A
9 Strathkildonan Gold	A
10 Forsinard	C
11 Rosehall Forest Trails & Falls	B
12 South Loch Fleet	C
13 Raven's Rock Gorge	C
14 Ferry Wood	C
15 Ord Hill	C
16 Falls of Shin	C
17 Skelbo Sculpture Trail	C
18 Dornoch Point	B
19 Dornoch & Embo	B
20 Ledmore & Migdale	B
21 Achue	B
22 Loch Fleet & Littleferry	C/B
23 The Duke of Sutherland	B
24 Above Strath Brora	A
25 Brora to Golspie	B
26 Big Burn	C

Five Short Walks

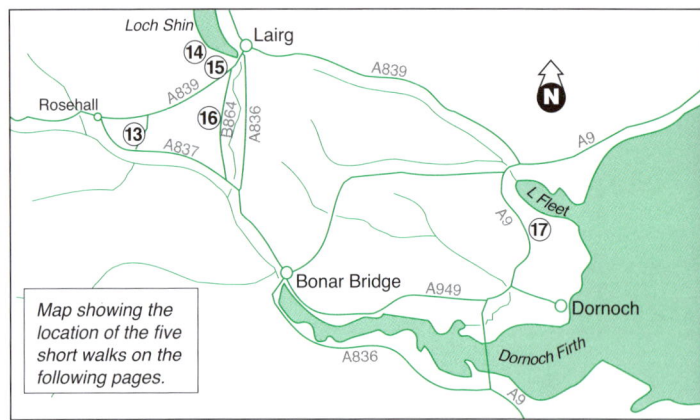

Map showing the location of the five short walks on the following pages.

13 Raven's Rock Gorge _____ C

Two short there-and-back waymarked forest walks exploring a little wooded valley. Length: up to **1 mile/1.6km**; Height Climbed: **130ft/40m**.

The car park for this walk lies on the minor road linking the A839 (the road running west from Lairg) and the A837, close to their junction near Rosehall.

A map in the car park shows the two routes. This walk used to be a circuit, but a major landslip in the narrow part of the valley has cut the connection.

The two walks start together, then split. The shorter, red route, descends into the pleasant valley, full of beech, birch and conifers. Look out for the bear (fortunately just a wood-carving!).

The blue route leads through the woods above the gorge to reach two viewpoints looking down to the river below.

Beinn a' Bhragaidh, behind Golspie, is climbed when visiting the dramatic monument to the Duke of Sutherland (*23*).

Natural Arch at Strathy Point (see Walk 2)

Walks explore the full range of the area's varied coastal scenery; from the high cliffs and stacks of Strathy Point in the north (*2*), to the muddy tidal basin of Loch Fleet (*12,22*) and the long sand spit of Dornoch Point (*18*) in the south.

The region's forests and woodlands are extensive and full of interest. There are fine woodland walks in Migdale (*20,21*) and at Rosehall (*11*), and interesting shorter walks through the trees at Skelbo (*17*), Falls of Shin (*16*), Raven's Rock Gorge (*13*) and Big Burn, at Golspie (*26*).

Inland areas are largely covered by moorland, including vast areas of wet moorland dotted with small lochans – the 'flow country' (*10*). Clear paths and tracks are scarce on the moors, but the walks chosen make use of them where possible.

Many walks will appeal to those interested in the area's natural history, the routes at Strathy Point (*2*), Forsinard (*10*) and Loch Fleet (*12,22*) being particularly good for birdwatching. Sutherland's ancient history is illustrated by the cairns and hut circles on Ord Hill (*15*), and the remains of brochs (circular fortified dwellings) passed on a number of routes (*5,14,25*).

Plenty of time should be allowed for all the walks, not only for exploration, but because many of the walks are rough underfoot and not always on paths. Mountain walks, and those traversing wild country, should only be undertaken with an eye on the weather (which can change very quickly!) and with the appropriate equipment and standard of fitness.

1 Melvich Bay

Melvich Bay forms the estuary of the Halladale River and is an area worth exploring, so allow plenty of time. The walking is rough in places, visiting the dunes before rounding the bay to the old pier and returning through the village of Melvich. Dogs must be kept under close control at all times. Length: **3 miles/5km**; *Height Climbed:* **200ft/60m**. *NB: This walk may be restricted by high tides.*

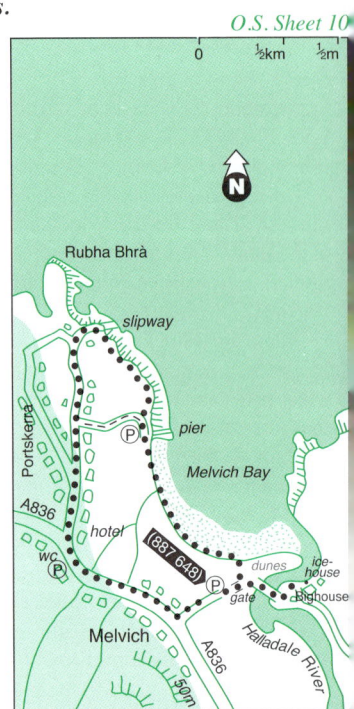

Melvich lies at the north-east extremity of the area covered by this guide, at the northern end of Strath Halladale.

From the A836 in the village of Melvich drive down the very narrow road signposted 'Melvich Beach'. This ends at a car park. Take the path signposted 'Footpath to Melvich Beach'. Just beyond the gate the path splits. First take the right-hand path, over the bridge, to explore the old icehouse that lies just past Bighouse.

Return to the split and this time take the other path from the gate, north towards the beach. This goes through the dunes then suddenly emerges onto a beautiful expanse of unspoilt beach. Turn left along the beach and follow what becomes a rough path at the upper edge of the beach all the way to the pier below Portskerra.

Walk up the road for 100m from the pier to a car park where there is a memorial to 'The Portskerra Drownings' (the route can be shortened here by going straight up the road from the pier).

Just past the car park take the path signposted 'Portskerra Slipway ½ mile'. Follow this path, marked by posts, along the cliffs to the slipway.

Turn left up the road then left again through the village of Portskerra to reach the A836. Turn left here to return to Melvich.

2 Strathy Point _____ B

This walk explores the spectacular headland of Strathy Point, with its towering cliffs and magnificent natural arches. Although short, the walking is quite rough. Allow time for exploration, and to study the wild flowers and birdlife. **NB: This walk is unsuitable for small children unless kept under close control in the vicinity of the cliffs.** *Dogs on leads. Length:* about **3 miles/5km**; *Height Climbed:* undulating.

O.S. Sheet 10

The village of Strathy lies 10 miles east of Bettyhill on the A836. To the north, Strathy Point juts out into the sea with a lighthouse at its tip. At the village, turn on to a minor road which leads up the eastern edge of the peninsula. This ends at a car park.

Walk in a northerly direction from the car park, through a gate, past a house, turning left on the metalled road that leads to the lighthouse.

Leave the road and head to the right of the lighthouse to explore (carefully) the tip of the point.

Double back from the point, crossing the road at the entrance to the lighthouse, and follow the edge of the cliffs roughly south-west, mostly on sheep tracks and keeping to the cliff side of the fence. Note the spectacular natural arches, islets and geos, but take great care!

When the fence turns left follow it, keeping the fence on your left, to ascend Druim Allt a' Mhuilinn. Note the magnificent views: to the west over Cape Wrath, and east, beyond Dounreay, to Orkney.

At the top of the hill bypass the OS trig point, which is on the other side of the fence. A little further on the fence turns left again. Follow it

Lighthouse on Strathy Point

downhill for about 300m to a gate. At this point the fence bends to the left and here you leave it, heading to the right at about 45° to reach the corner of another fenced area, about 250m away over rough ground.

Keep this fence on the left and follow a rough path for about 100m to reach a farm track that leads back to the road. Turn left on the road to return to the car park.

3 Armadale to Poulouriscaig ————————————————— B

A short, lineal walk on rough tracks and paths, leading across moorland to an abandoned settlement. Length: **3 miles/5km** *(there and back); Height climbed:* **560ft/170m** *(undulating).*

O.S. Sheet 10

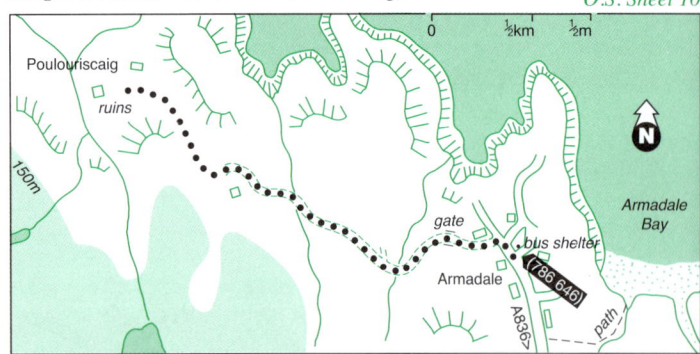

The little north coast settlement of Armadale is six miles east of Bettyhill on a signposted spur road running north from the A836. As you drive along this road you will notice a signpost to your right for the beach at Armadale Bay. This is a fine sand beach and well worth exploring if you have the time.

A little under a mile from the junction with the A836 the road splits at an old bus shelter. Park to the right (being careful not to block access) and walk down the left-hand road.

After a short distance you reach a white/yellow house to the left of the road, on the near side of which the signposted track to Poulouriscaig begins.

The track passes through a gate then descends to cross a small burn. As it begins to climb beyond the burn it splits. Keep left.

After crossing a second burn the track zig-zags up a steeper slope to pass to the right of a square structure, visible on the horizon. At the top of this slope the built-up track ends. Walk straight on, into a little transverse valley, in which you should see a post with an arrow on it, pointing right.

Go in the direction indicated, following a rough path down the right-hand side of the valley, before crossing over and climbing briefly to reach the edge of the ruined township.

Poulouriscaig was settled in the early 19th century by people cleared from more fertile land to the south. It was inhabited for around a century, but all that remains now are a few ruined buildings.

Return by the same route.

4 Around Bettyhill_____B

A fine short walk with outstanding views and a magnificent beach. Allow plenty of time to visit the Strathnaver Museum, which gives an insight into the Highland Clearances. **Length: 4 miles/6.5km**; *Height climbed:* undulating.

O.S. Sheet 10

Strathnaver Museum

This walk starts from the museum/café car park adjacent to the main A836 road at the east end of Bettyhill.

Walk west from the car park towards the village along the main road. After 400m turn right onto a minor road signposted for Farr Beach. (Note the start of the footpath to the beach on the right.) Follow the road to a T-junction at its conclusion. To the right at this point is an old salmon fishing station; to the left the pier.

Double back to the start of the Farr Beach path. Turn left here, through a kissing gate, and follow the path to the beach.

Walk to the far end of the beach and climb a steep grassy bank to join a footpath. Turn left and follow the path along the side of the headland to reach a gate in a fence, beyond which it is a short climb to a low hilltop marked by a cairn.

The views are superb. Looking along the headland you will see two further low hills (the second marked by a cairn), then the low ground of the point beyond. Explore as far as you wish.

Follow the path back to the end of the beach but this time keep straight on, through dunes. When the path reaches a gate (with a path signposted for Farr Bay joining from the right) go through and continue.

Continue until you reach a kissing gate on your right, opposite a well-built wall. Go through this and turn left on the main track to reach the road. Turn right to return to the start.

5 Invernaver Nature Reserve & Broch   B

A short but rough walk across a nature reserve to the remains of a broch in a stunning location overlooking the estuary of the River Naver and Bettyhill. **Length: 3 miles/4.5km** *(there and back);* **Height Climbed: 400ft/120m.** *Possible alternative return through the dunes.* O.S. Sheet 10

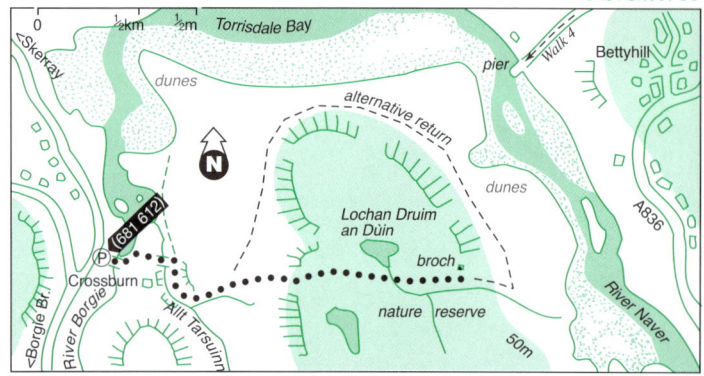

To reach the start of this walk, turn north from Borgie Bridge (6 miles west of Bettyhill on the A836) onto the minor road to Skerray. After around 1½ miles the road forks. Go right here and, after 200m, there is a car park on your right.

At the north end of the car park there is a sign for Torrisdale Beach. Follow the path down steps and over the River Borgie by a footbridge, then continue to cross the Allt Tarsuinn by a smaller footbridge.

A turn to the left beyond the bridge leads down to the beach, but for this walk turn right, up the glen of the burn, with a cottage (Crossburn) high on the right.

The path curves round to the left, keeping to the left of a gate then climbing away from the burn up a bank of gorse. The path now becomes indistinct. Looking ahead you will see a steep slope of heather and rock, with a line of electricity poles climbing it. The rough path follows the line of the poles.

The path passes Lochan Druim an Dùin and begins to descend. If you look up to your left you will see the remains of the broch (a fortified dwelling) on a rocky outcrop. This is a magnificent viewpoint.

The quickest return is by the same route. Alternatively, you can take the steep path down to the dunes and turn left to go around the headland. You may choose to visit the broad beach (tide allowing), but the clearest return is along the inside of the dunes.

6 Ben Loyal — A+

The isolated Ben Loyal gives the impression of a daunting climb. However, there should be no real difficulties for experienced hillwalkers – providing the climb is only attempted in clear weather. **NB: The burn may be difficult to cross if in spate.** *Length:* **9 miles/14km** (there and back); *Height Climbed:* **2750ft/840m**.

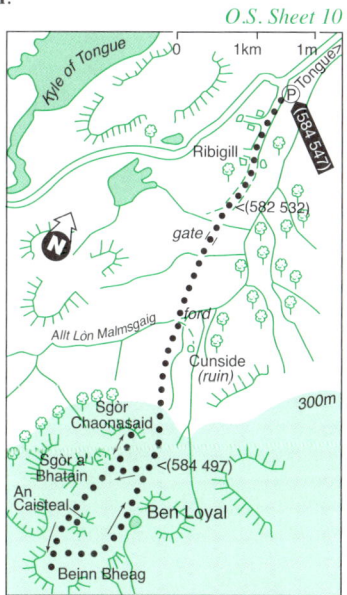

Drive south on a minor road from Tongue. After a mile the road passes a monument. Just beyond this it splits: keep left. Almost immediately there is a car park to the left of the road, just before a cattle grid.

Walk past the cattle grid and on. After a short distance you pass a bungalow and the road forks. Keep left. Almost immediately there is a second split, at the farmyard. Keep left again, through the farmyard, then continue along a rough track.

The track leads through a gate in a fence then over rough moorland. If you lose the path here, look ahead to the ford over Allt Lòn Malmsgaig, to the right of Cunside, and aim for that.

The path goes up the right-hand side of the burn beyond and on, diagonally, up the hillside to emerge at a flattish boggy area (584 497). From here bear right and go up steep, grassy slopes, making for the col between Sgòr Chaonasaid and Sgòr a' Bhatain.

Once on the col turn right to visit the summit of Sgòr Chaonasaid. Double back from here and head for the west (right-hand) side of the main summit tor, An Caisteal. The path goes left and ascends rocks (take care here) for a short way as the main summit is approached.

After enjoying the magnificent views, retrace the first 50m or so from the summit and turn left to head for the second col and third summit at spot height 744m (Beinn Bheag).

Return to the second col and bear right diagonally down steep slopes to regain the flat boggy area. Retrace the outward route from here.

7 Ben Klibreck _____ A+

Ben Klibreck, standing alone above the village of Altnaharra, is the only Munro in east Sutherland. Two alternative routes are shown; the steeper more direct path can be difficult to identify from below, so it is better to climb Creag an Lochain on the ascent. Keep this walk for a clear day.
Length: **8½ miles/13.5km**; *Height Climbed:* **2900ft/880m**. O.S. Sheet 16

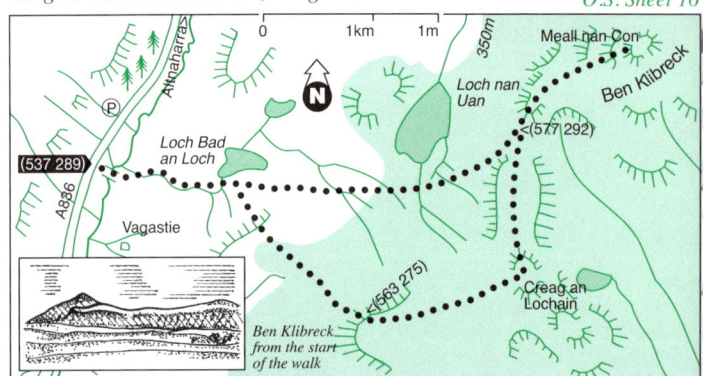

Drive 4 miles south from Altnaharra on the A836. There is limited roadside parking ½ mile north of the cottage at Vagastie. (Avoid blocking passing places: there is a larger car park about ¾ mile further north.)

Cross the road and go over the footbridge. The path follows the right-hand side of a little burn. Cross the burn to pass through a gate at the end of a fence, then cross it again about 20m before the outlet from Loch Bad an Loch. Turn right and continue on an ever more vague path towards the hill.

Turn right and head for the shoulder just to the left of the col to the west of Creag an Lochain. The shoulder is reached around Grid Ref 563 275. The route then curves round to the left and heads up to the summit of Creag an Lochain.

From here a grand ridge walk crosses the final col at 577 292 before ascending, with Ben Klibreck's only real crags on the left, to the foot of the final rocky slope up to the main summit.

After enjoying the superb views from the top, retrace your steps and descend to the previous col (577 292). From here a descending traverse goes right, taking an easy line across steep ground (there are two paths; either will do). These paths lead onto very rough but less steep ground, eventually rejoining the outward route.

Return by the same route.

8 Loch Badanloch & Creag an Alltan Fheàrna ___ A

This walk traverses wild country typical of inland east Sutherland: an area of wild lochs and little-frequented heather-clad hills. The hill section, unsurprisingly, is pathless, but the route takes advantage of estate tracks for much of the distance. The views are extensive rather than spectacular, giving a 'feel' of what east Sutherland's wild country is about. Length: **10 miles/16km**; *Height Climbed:* **650ft/200m**.

O.S. Sheets 16 & 17

NB: *This is an active stalking estate. In late summer and autumn, please look out for notices regarding stalking activity and act as requested. (Stalking does not take place on Sundays).*

The start of the walk lies on the B871 road about 5 miles west of Kinbrace, which itself is on the A897 road running north-west from Helmsdale.

Park by the barrier at the start of the track near Badanloch Lodge. Take care not to obstruct the track as it is in regular use by the estate and for fishing access.

Go through the barrier and along the track towards Loch Badanloch. Cross over two bridges and continue until (at Grid Ref 779 327) a rougher track leads off to the left, through a gate, towards a building. Follow this. The track ends at the building but a rough path continues beyond.

The path descends then begins to climb again. As you approach the highest point of the path turn right, off the path and onto the trackless hill, heading all the time for the rising ground that leads along the ridge of Creag an Alltan Fheàrna. The ground is boggy with tussocks but is punctuated by orchids and a variety of bog plants. Eventually the summit is reached (747 321), giving extensive views of some very remote and wild country.

Descend a grassy spur (slightly west of due north) aiming, initially, for the west shore of Loch Rimsdale, until the broad descending ridge comes into full view.

The main track is reached around 745 331, turn right here and follow the track to rejoin the outward route.

9 Strathkildonan Gold — A

The discovery of gold in the Kildonan Burn led to a modest 'Gold Rush' in the Strath of Kildonan in 1868-9. The small quantities involved made the business of prospecting uneconomic, but people still pan the River Helmsdale and its tributaries for gold dust with some success.

This walk explores some of the old workings before ascending Cnoc na Béiste and traversing the wild country above the glens of the Suisgill and Kildonan Burns. Most of the walk is on paths and tracks but there is a rough cross-country section after Cnoc na Béiste. Length: **9 miles/ 14km**; *Height Climbed:* **950ft/290m**.

O.S. Sheet 17

This walk lies in the middle of the Strath of Kildonan, which runs north-west from Helmsdale to Kinbrace.

12 miles from Helmsdale (and 5 miles from Kinbrace) the A897 crosses the Suisgill Burn. Just west of the crossing point there is limited roadside parking to the south side of the road (Grid Ref 895 252 – do not park by the house).

Head east along the road for around 250m then turn left onto open ground, just past the house and before the new and old road bridges. Continue past the sheep pens to a bridge not marked on the OS map (898 254). Cross this and continue up the east bank of the Suisgill Burn on a grassy track with a circular sheep fank on the right.

The old gold workings can be seen around 905 269, at which point cross the burn and head up the heather- and bracken-covered spur at the far side. At first the faint track goes straight up Cnoc na Béiste, but then it bears left and starts to level off. Here, strike up to the right over rough ground, heading directly for the top of the hill and ignoring a few random 'quad bike' tracks.

Take a rest by the small cairn that marks the summit and enjoy the fine views of the conical peak of Morven, to the east (in Caithness), then head just south of due east (just to the right of Morven) across rough ground. Aim for the end of the contour track on Torr nan Gabhar. Resist the temptation to short-cut to the right: this will lead to the crossing of two ravines and a climb to reach the track.

Once the end of the track has been located it is an easy high-level traverse across Torr nan Gabhar and Cnoc a' Mheadhoin. The track then descends; passing over a bridge, under power lines and down a steep zig-zag to emerge on the road at Suisgill Lodge. Turn right to return to your parking place.

10 Forsinard _____ C

A short circular walk on a boardwalk and a flagstone path, to an impressive viewing tower overlooking the 'Flow Country' – the landscape of peat bogs and pools on the Sutherland/Caithness border. Additional information is available from the excellent visitor centre, run by the RSPB in the old Forsinard railway station building. **No dogs please.** *Length:* **1 mile/1.6km**; *Height Climbed:* none.

Forsinard lies on the single-track A897 Strath Halladale road between Kinbrace and Melvich.

Park in the car park opposite the station and, after visiting the display area in the station, walk south down the road (ie, turn left on leaving the visitor centre). The boardwalk Dubh Lochan Trail is signposted to your right just beyond the level-crossing.

Follow the Trail to the impressive viewing tower overlooking the peat bogs, then follow the Flagstone Trail back to the road.

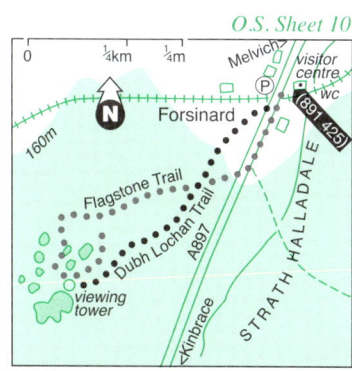

O.S. Sheet 10

11 Rosehall Forest Trails & Falls B

Rosehall Forest Trails provide a variety of short forest walks from the information hut and car park. The walk below uses a compilation of the waymarked routes to form a longer walk, exploring more of the forest and visiting a fine waterfall. Length: **5½ miles/9km**; *Height Climbed:* up to **425ft/130m**.

O.S. Sheet 16

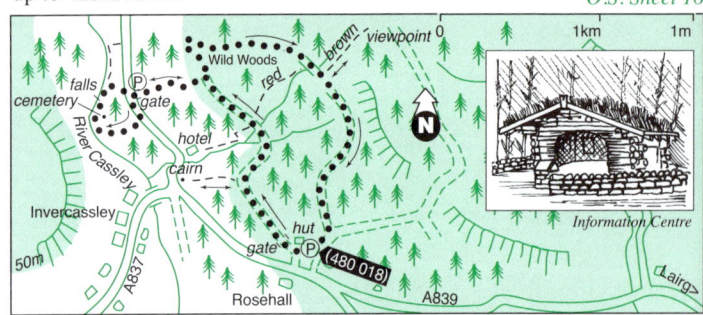

The car park for this walk is on the A837, just west of its junction with the A839 (the road running west from Lairg). The walks through the forest are colour-coded and waymarked.

Look for the clear track which heads west from the car park (green/yellow/red). Follow this through a gate and continue. After a short distance a signposted path heads off to the left (green). This marks the start of a possible diversion to the 'Millennium Cairn' (*see* map). If you are not doing this, continue along the main track. Just beyond a stone bridge, the red trail heads off to the right (*see* map). For this walk, however, keep straight on along the main track.

When you reach a sign for the Wild Woods the path splits. Go left (green) on the smaller path, which drops down to a gate by the public road. Go through the gate and turn left. At the first passing place go right, through a field gate, then cross the field (livestock) to reach the river.

Turn right and follow the riverbank past the falls, keeping the cemetery on your right. When you reach a wooden gate across the path, go right to rejoin the road, then follow your original route back up to the junction by the Wild Woods.

To complete the circuit, turn left (yellow). The track runs across the slope for a short way before doubling back and climbing. The route back to the car park is well signposted, and there is one possibility for a diversion. Just after crossing a burn, a brown post to your left marks the start of a steep climb to a good viewpoint.

12 South Loch Fleet _____ C

The Loch Fleet National Nature Reserve lies between Dornoch and Golspie. This short walk explores the south side of the Loch (see also walk 22). This is an excellent walk for bird watchers and those interested in spotting seals, which are often basking on sandbanks or rocks near the shore. Lovers of wild flowers will find plenty of interest in June and July. **NB: Dogs must be kept under close control at all times.** *Length:* about **2-3 miles/3-5km** (there and back); *Height Climbed:* negligible.

O.S. Sheet 21

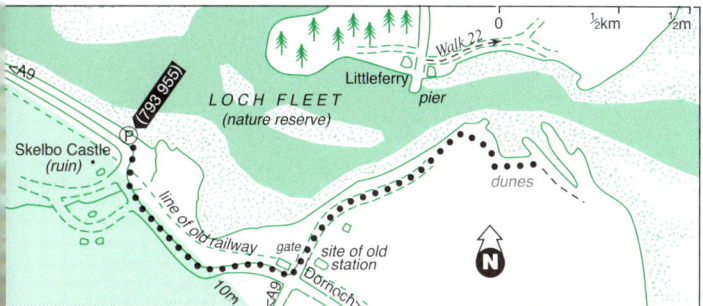

Loch Fleet is a tidal basin at the mouth of the River Fleet: all that remains of what was once a larger estuary stretching some miles up the valley of the Fleet. The mound carrying the road at the western end of the loch was built in 1816 by Thomas Telford, and once carried the now disused Dornoch Railway.

The loch is now protected as a nature reserve. The basin, drying and flooding twice every day, is a great place for spotting wildfowl and waders (ospreys can also be seen between April and August), while the dunes surrounding the mouth of the loch are of equal interest.

Access to the start of this route is from the minor road linking Dornoch and Embo. Park at the Reserve car park, just across the road from the ruin of Skelbo Castle.

Walk along the minor road from the Reserve car park and turn left at the four-way crossroads, passing through a gate and continuing along a rough track. Note the old station platform, a relic of the old Dornoch Railway, on your right. Head out to the end of the track and continue beyond on paths to the area of dunes opposite Littleferry. **NB: Be careful not to get cut off by the tide, which fills the long inlets surprisingly quickly!**

Return by the same route.

Walks East Sutherland

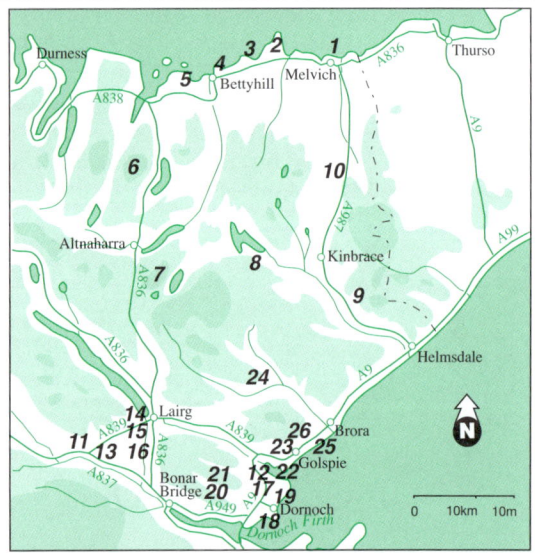

Grades

A+ .... Full walking equipment – including map and compass – and previous hill walking experience essential

A ...... Full walking equipment required

B ...... Strong walking footwear and waterproof clothing required

C ...... Comfortable walking footwear recommended

[B/C, etc ...... Split grades mean that the route described can be walked either in its entirety or in shorter, less gruelling sections.**]**

NB: Assume each walk increases at least one grade in winter conditions. Hill routes can become treacherous.

www.pocketwalks.com

Published by: Hallewell Publications, Scotland
Printed by: Barr Printers, Glenrothes

While every care has been taken in the preparation of this guide, the publishers cannot accept responsibility for any loss, damage or injury resulting from its use.

14 Ferry Wood / 15 Ord Hill _____ C/C

Two short routes starting from the Ferrycroft Countryside Centre (closed in winter) on the western edge of Lairg. **Walk 14)** *A circular, waymarked forest walk visiting the remains of a broch (circular fortified dwelling) on the shore of Loch Shin. Easy, well-made paths throughout. Watch out for the wood-carved animals near the wildlife pond. Length:* **1¹/₂ miles/2km**; *Height Climbed: negligible.* **Walk 15)** *A short hill walk with open views over Lairg. This route is of particular archaeological interest, as it visits ancient cairns and hut circles. Length:* **1¹/₂ miles/2km**; *Height Climbed:* **250ft/75m**.

O.S. Sheet 16

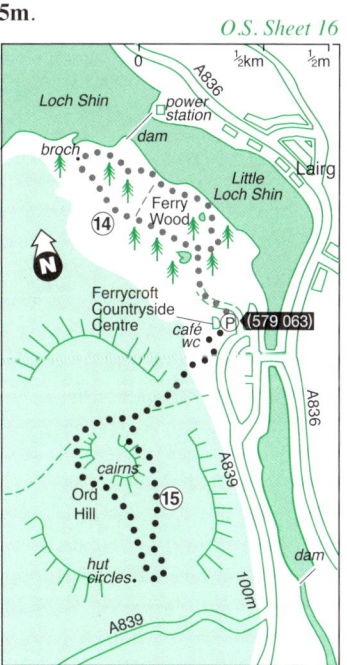

Lairg is a small village at the southern end of Loch Shin. It straddles the River Shin, linked by the road bridge carrying the A839. On the western side of the river you will find the Ferrycroft Countryside Centre. This is the starting point for both these walks, and is well worth a visit on its own account.

Walk 14) Park by the Countryside Centre. Leave the car park following the clear track between the centre and the playing fields. When the track ends, carry straight on, through a gate following a clear path (green/red markers). The route is perfectly clear and can be followed in either direction, through the woods by Little Loch Shin, up to the ruined broch above Loch Shin, and back to the car park. The shorter (red) route omits the broch (*see* map).

Walk 15) Walk left along the front of the building to find a sign for the start of the Ord Hill walk.

The path heads towards the mound of Ord Hill then splits. Keep right and follow the clear path to the top of the hill, passing the sites of hut circles and other antiquities. After enjoying the fine views, continue on a clear, rough path, which soon doubles back to complete the loop.

16 Falls of Shin _____C

Three short forest walks; two involving some uphill walking and one viewing the River Shin and Shin Falls, where you may see salmon leaping as they swim up the river (Feb–Sep). Length: up to 1¼ mile/2km (green route); Height Climbed: up to 170ft/50m.

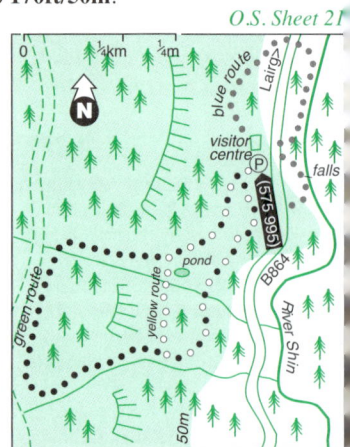

O.S. Sheet 21

The start of these walks is at the Falls of Shin Visitor Centre, 4 miles south of Lairg on the B864 (the road running south from Lairg down the *west* side of the River Shin).

The Shin is a famous salmon river, and the first thing you should do is to cross the road and follow the steps and steep paths to the riverside to the point overlooking the falls. With luck, you may see some fish.

The two longer waymarked walks (the Woodland Trail and the Pond & Play Trail), climbing into the forest, are easy to follow and the routes are never in doubt. They may be walked in either direction.

17 Skelbo Sculpture Trail _____C

Skelbo Wood is great for children. The walk is enhanced by wooden sculptures along the way that are great fun to spot. The walk is in pleasant woodland descending to a burn before climbing back up to the start. Length: 1½ miles/2km; Height Climbed: 200ft/60m.

O.S. Sheet 21

Skelbo Wood is situated just off the A9, about 6 miles north of the bridge over the Dornoch Firth. The car park is clearly signposted from the road.

The walk is clearly waymarked, following green marker posts in a clockwise circuit. Look out for the remains of an old broch (a circular fortified dwelling), and of course for the wooden sculptures.

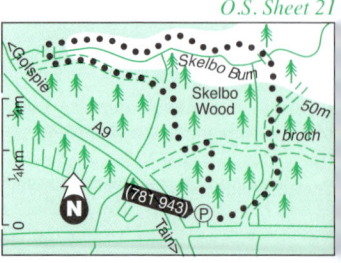

18 Dornoch Point_____B

An easy walk exploring the coast and sand dunes south of Dornoch, starting from the main square. Those interested in wild flowers and birdlife will enjoy this area. **NB: This walk may not be possible at high tide so check tide times in advance at** http://www.ukho.gov.uk/easytide/EasyTide **and don't get yourself cut off!** *Length:* **4 miles/6km**; *Height Climbed:* none.

O.S. Sheet 21

Leave the main square by Church Street (signposted for the Beach). Follow this, passing the Free Church, to reach an interpretive panel about the 'Littletown Rents and Refugees' by a junction.

Continue straight on (River Street). At the end of the houses, go right on to a tarmac road across the golf links (beware of golf balls!).

When you reach Dornoch Landing Strip car park turn left and pick up a path at the far side of the car park. This runs along the line of posts that marks the landing strip boundary and heads for the dunes.

Walk through the dunes to reach the beach then turn right and follow it to Dornoch Point. (**NB:** if the tide is high, follow the paths through the dunes and double back if in doubt.)

You can return from the Point by your original route. If you feel adventurous, however, look for a rough path heading right when the dunes end to your right. A series of faint paths cross the salt marshes behind the dunes to rejoin your outward path by the landing strip. **Please note that this area will flood at high tide, so take care.**

NB: *A series of rough paths leads back across the salt marshes behind the dunes. Some navigation will be needed, but the landing strip should alway be visible. The area will be covered at high tide, so ensure you are aware of tide times.*

19 Dornoch & Embo   B

A fine coastal circuit north of Dornoch. It covers some magnificent areas of gorse, so is at its best in May and June. The walk runs beside golf links (beware of golf balls!), and along a rocky stretch of coastline and an old railway line. **Length: 6 miles/9km**; *Height Climbed:* negligible. *Some care needed with navigation at the start.*

O.S. Sheet 21

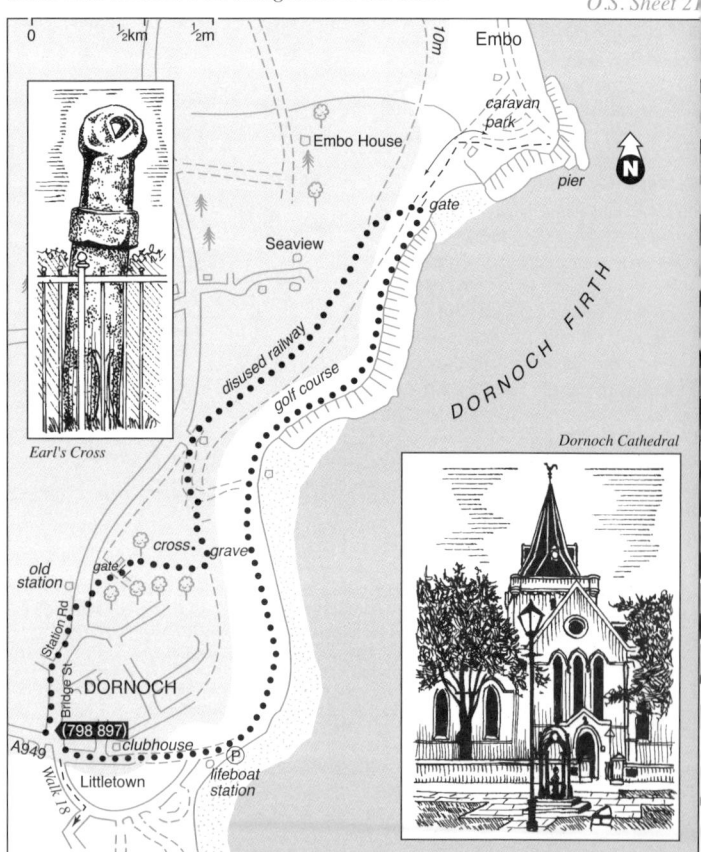

20 Ledmore & Migdale / 21 Achue — B/B

20) *A connected network of four waymarked walks through fine mixed woodland, leading to spectacular views over the Dornoch Firth and Loch Migdale. Length:* **1-4½ miles/1.5-7km**; *Height Climbed:* up to **490ft/150m** (on A' Chraisg route). **21)** *A connected (but un-waymarked) circuit on the northern side of the glen, passing through splendid mixed woodland and giving a view over the moors. Length:* **3½ miles/6km**; *Height Climbed:* **390ft/120m**.

O.S. Sheet 21

Walk 20
- • • • Loch Migdale
- • • • A' Chraisg
- ○ ○ ○ ○ Honest George's Circuit
- ◎ ◎ ◎ ◎ Spinningdale View

Walk 21
- ■ ■ ■ ■ Achue

From the main square in Dornoch, head up the left side of Bridge Street. This leads into Station Road, with the river just to your left.

A short distance before the brightly-painted old station building, cross the road and go up the steps on the right, signposted for Embo. The path forks immediately. Keep left, following the path running parallel to the road. After a short distance this swings right, up through the trees, before heading left with a fence to its left.

At a kissing gate, cross the road and go straight on: signposted 'Earl's Cross Wood'. Continue with a fence and a timber house on your left. When the grounds of the house end there is a green and brown post and the path splits. Bear left here and follow the path (and posts) down through the wood.

The path runs along the bottom of the wood, then pulls away from the field, in a stand of conifers, and quickly reaches a fork marked by a post with a red ring round it. Take the right-hand path, marked by a yellow arrow. This quickly leads to an old grave, marked by an interpretative panel. You are now in an area of mixed woodland and gorse,

Thirty paces after the panel the path forks. Keep left here (yellow arrow). On this section you will pass Earl's Cross, which lies just off the main path, to the left.

About 100m after the Cross you reach a junction. Keep straight on here (left-hand path), passing through what used to be a gate and continuing through dense gorse, with the golf course now down to your right.

The path drops down to a gravel road. If you went right here you would cross the golf course, but for this route go left. After ten paces you reach a T-junction with another path. Go right.

This brings you up to a junction, with a house to your right. Go right here (Embo). You are now walking along the old railway line. Looking ahead, you will be able to see the white mass of Embo House in a stand of trees, and the sharp point of the Sutherland Monument on its hill behind Golspie (*see* Walk 23).

Just after you pass the buildings at Seaview, up to your left, the path splits. Go right, dropping down to go around the far end of the golf course. If you pass through the pedestrian gate here, a short walk will lead you to the campsite on the edge of Embo. Otherwise, simply double back between the golf course and the shore. (For your own safety, and out of courtesy to the players, please keep a close eye on any shots being played as you walk by.)

You may need to make a diversion onto the beach at one point. If so, you can soon walk back through the dunes and pick up a clear track. When this reaches the 16th tee it turns inland, towards a car park. Walk through this and past the lifeboat station beyond. Just beyond this there is a junction. Keep straight on, past the clubhouse and back to the town square.

of the bridge turn left yet again, onto Harbour Road, and go under the railway bridge.

50m after the railway bridge take the path down to the left, to the river's edge, noting the old ice-house on the right. At the end of the harbour side go up the ramp to regain the road. Turn left along this to continue.

Keep left, past the picnic benches, keeping to the road nearest the shoreline. On reaching Salt Street, turn left (after the cottages on the left) signposted 'Beach Car Park'. Go straight through the car park towards the flat-roofed buildings that lie ahead. Half way between the car park and these buildings bear left on a track, keeping the beach immediately to the left.

The path continues close to the beach to the left of the fence. A little over a mile/1.6km from Brora a slightly awkward section drops down steeply through gorse to the beach, just before the picturesque waterfall formed by the Sputie Burn.

There are extensive views south to Tarbat Ness lighthouse and, on a clear day, the Cairngorms.

Continue with the beach on the left. Dunrobin Castle comes into view about half a mile/0.8km before the remains of the broch (a circular fortified dwelling) are reached. The main path passes close to the broch but any one of a number of paths will lead on below Dunrobin.

(Dunrobin Castle, the ancestral home of the Earls and Dukes of Sutherland, is the largest house in the north of Scotland. Parts of it date back at least to the early 15th century, but its current appearance – more like a French château than what one thinks of as a Scottish castle – is due to the work of Sir Charles Barry (architect of the Palace of Westminster), who remodelled the castle in the mid-19th century. The castle gardens are open to the public all year; the building itself from April to October.)

100m after entering the wood the track forks by a red and green marker post. Take the track on the left, passing a similar post.

After a clearing, keep left on a smaller path through a thicket. This emerges on a track that goes past the walled grounds of the castle and on to more open ground.

As Golspie is approached, go through a field with the first houses visible ahead. As you approach them, edge right to reach a gate, then keep straight on to cross a footbridge over the Golspie Burn.

At the far end of the bridge turn left, crossing a track leading to a ford, and go down a metalled road. Keep straight on to a path, with the sea always to the left. This path eventually becomes a road.

Continue, the road becoming a path again, until a car park is reached. (Any of the side streets on the right lead to the main road).

Turn right through the car park to reach the main A9. Turn left along this and the station is reached in about 400m, on the left-hand side of the main road.

26 Big Burn

A series of well-made linked paths running up a fine, narrow, wooded den and visiting a picturesque waterfall. Leave plenty of time to explore.
NB: This walk is unsuitable for young children unless they are under close control. *Length:* **1½-2½ miles/2-4km**; *Height Climbed:* up to **200ft/60m**.

O.S. Sheet 17

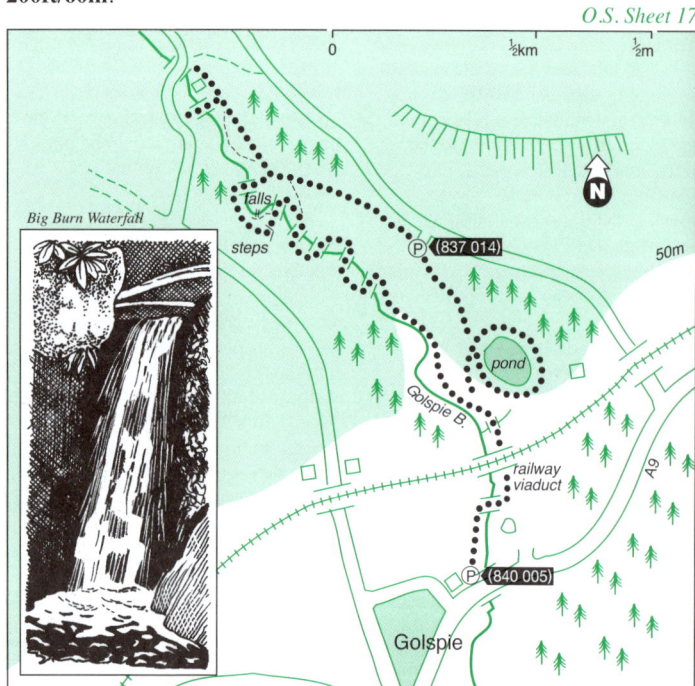

There are two parking places for Big Burn. The first is at the lower end of the burn, adjacent to Sutherland Stonework Monumental Masons (look carefully for the 'Car Park' sign!). This is the start of a walk going under the railway bridge, up to the falls and returning via the high-level path and the skating pond.

The high-level car park is situated up the minor road on the north side of the burn. This gives easy access to the pond, with the option of extending the walk to the falls (*see map*).

The River Brora runs from the wild country of the Ben Armine Forest, south-east of Ben Klibreck (*see* Walk 7), to the town of Brora on the east coast of Sutherland (*see* Walk 25).

Access to the river's lower strath is by a minor road that runs from Rogart, in Strath Fleet, to Brora. This walk starts from just north of Dalreavoch (5 miles north of Rogart; 13 miles from Brora). There is limited space to park at the entry to a disused forest track.

From here, walk south along the minor road and turn right up the first track, about 75m before the bridge over the River Brora. After 25m take a rough, grassy track leading off on the right, up the left-hand side of the wood. A smaller group of trees lies to the left.

After the end of the smaller group of trees is cleared, the path is joined by a slightly better path coming up from the left, from an iron gate at the boundary of Dalreavoch Lodge. Keep going uphill, through a gate by the top corner of the wood and onto the open hillside beyond. Continue on the path, passing Loch Grùdaidh on your right-hand side.

As you approach a gate, the path forks. Go right here, through the gate, and continue on the rough path which then passes to the right of Loch Beannach. The path becomes somewhat vague as it passes another iron gate and Lochan Dubh (clear on the OS, but unseen from the path).

You are now descending, across a slope, with Loch Bad an t-Sean-tighe visible down to your left. Just beyond the far end of the loch a plank bridge crosses the burn (NB: this bridge is in poor condition at time of writing and you may prefer to ford the burn). Beyond that there is no clear path, but you should see a deer fence just ahead. Aim for the gate in this fence.

Beyond the gate a heathery track runs straight through an area of conifers. At the far end of the plantation there is a second gate, beyond which you join a clear track running down the glen of the Black Water.

Turn right along this track. The track re-crosses the Allt a' Mhuilinn Duibh by a bridge. At the far side of the bridge keep to the right-hand track and head up to the skyline.

Another area of lochans (and glacial drumlins) is passed before entering the forest. Keep straight on through the forest, ignoring tracks cutting off to right and left. The track becomes metalled as it skirts around Sciberscross Lodge.

When the road is reached turn right and follow it for $1^1/_2$ miles/ 2.5km back to the start.

1 *Cnoc na Sguaibe* **2** *Cùl Beag* **3** *Cul Mor* **4** *Ben More Assynt* **5** *Glas Bheinn*

25 Brora to Golspie

This is a lineal coastal walk that explores an interesting stretch of North Sea coast between two railway stations. The best plan is to park at Golspie Station, catch the morning train to Brora, and walk south, enjoying the best views of Dunrobin Castle and the Duke of Sutherland's monument on Beinn a' Bhragaidh. The walk passes the remains of a broch, a waterfall and a castle, giving views of hills, coastline, and probably seals; what more could a walk offer? Length: **6½ miles/10km** (one way); *Height Climbed:* negligible.

O.S. Sheets 17 & 21

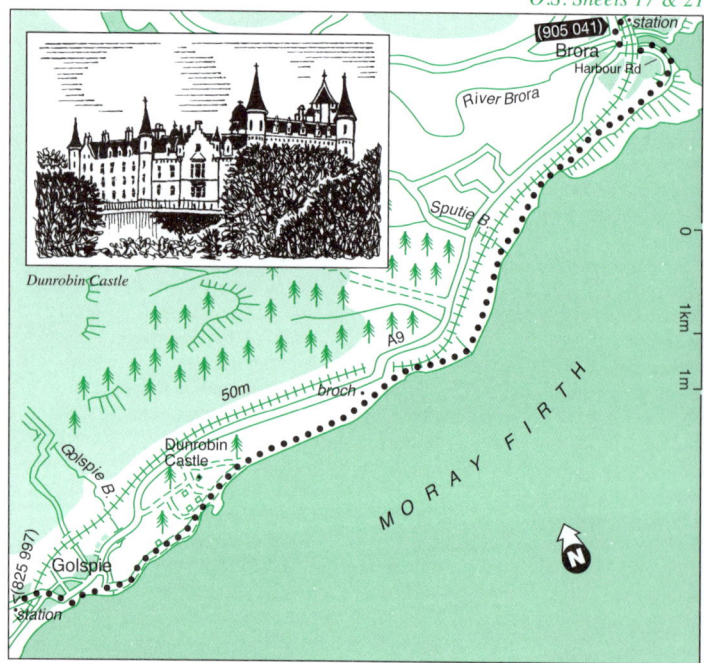

Leave the railway station at Brora, cross the station footbridge and head out onto the main road. (If parking in Brora, there is a car park immediately adjacent to the station car park).

Turn left on the main A9, cross the end of Golf Road and the bridge over the River Brora. At the far side

24 Above Strath Brora _____ A

After a short climb, this walk follows a path across wild country above Strath Brora, before returning on an estate track to the minor road. This has to be walked for about 1½ miles/2.5km to return to the car park. There is, therefore, no pathless walking. The route passes several fishing lochans and views are good throughout – even in the forest section.
Length: **11 miles/17km**; *Height Climbed:* **650ft/200m**.

O.S. Sheets 16 & 17

23 The Duke of Sutherland — B

The monument to the 1st Duke of Sutherland is situated on Beinn a' Bhragaidh, in a commanding position above Golspie. On a clear day it is visible from many points along the Sutherland coastline. This walk climbs up from Golspie, visits the monument, and descends by a different route. Parts of the ascent are quite steep. Length: **5 miles/8km**; Height Climbed: **1280ft/390m**.

O.S. Sheet 17

Park in Golspie at the junction of Fountain Road and the main street (A9). Walk (inland) up Fountain Road, past the church and the fountain, across the crossroads and under the railway: signposted for 'Ben Bhraggie'.

Continue past Rhives House and the track bears round to the right. 150m after the house turn left, signposted for Beinn a' Bhragaidh, onto a steep track through trees.

Just as the track swings off to the left, a rough path heads right, marked by a green arrow. Follow this up to a four-way junction. Keep straight on ('BBFP').

After fifty paces bear right, off the track, on to a signposted footpath. There are excellent views over Golspie from this point.

100m further on go under the power lines and, following the route of the wires, left for 100m. Emerge on a forest road (822 006). Cross this road and re-enter the forest by steps and a path at the far side. After another 100m cross yet another forest road, and re-enter the forest up more steps.

A steep ascent follows, with more steps, until a gate under a complex wooden structure leads onto open heather. Keep left beyond this and climb to the monument. The views are magnificent; especially of Loch Fleet, the Fearn peninsula and the Moray hills beyond.

Walk on away from the sea to pick up a track which gently descends before doubling back to re-enter the forest. Turn right when the main forest road is reached. Walk along this forest road as far as the power lines. Turn left here to retrace the route back to the start.

Ledmore and Migdale is an extensive area of woodland – a mixture of Scots pine, oak and birch – owned by Woodland Trust Scotland, in a picturesque glen to the north of the Dornoch Firth. The estate was once owned by the famous industrialist Andrew Carnegie, who lived at Skibo castle, a short distance to the east.

To reach the start of the walks, drive seven miles west from Dornoch on the A949/A9 to reach the little settlement of Spinningdale. Turn off the A949 at that point, on to the minor road signposted for Migdale. After a mile you will see a car park up a short access track to the right of the road.

Walks 20 & 21) There is an information board in the car park, and a box holding leaflets showing the routes. Immediately behind this a track starts, signposted for the routes. Follow the track a short distance to join the quiet public road, then start walking up the road.

After a short distance, a track starts to the left, marked by a Woodland Trust sign for the woods.

Walk 20) For the waymarked walks, turn left here.

For a low-level, lineal walk, follow the yellow markers through the pine woodland to the eastern end of Loch Migdale. The track continues along the northern side of the loch, eventually joining the end of the public road. It is a little over four miles/6.5km to the road end and back to the car park.

The other two routes are circuits, the longer being the climb up to the viewpoint on A' Chraisg.

A glance at the map will show the links between these routes and the fourth walk – a climb from Spinningdale to another viewpoint. A particular attraction of this walk is that it leads into the fine birch and oakwood overlooking the Dornoch Firth.

Walk 21) For the alternative route, keep straight on at the junction and continue along the public road. The road climbs, passing a white house, then levels out. When it does so, watch for an unmarked track heading back-right, starting opposite a lay-by.

Follow this clear track up and across the slope, until it levels out and there is open moorland beyond the fence to your left and pine woodland to your right.

The track passes the Red Dog Cairn (an archaeological site) then begins to descend. Watch for a track starting through a gate to your left. Ignore this and continue. Fifty paces further on a grassy track heads off to your right, marked by a waymark for a 'green' route.

Turn on to this path, which descends through mixed woodland to cross a burn on a footbridge. Continue descending beyond, watching for a fainter (waymarked) path heading off ahead-right. Turn on to this rough path. It leads down to a gate, and then on down the picturesque glen of a little burn.

At the foot of the glen, go through another gate to join the public road beside a bridge. Turn right to return to the car park.

22 Loch Fleet & Littleferry _____ C/B

Two undemanding walks by the side of tidal Loch Fleet. **A)** *A short lineal walk through woodland, leading to a bird hide. Length:* **2 miles/3km** *(there and back); Height Climbed: negligible.* **B)** *A circuit on multiple grassy paths through duneland to the north of the entry to the loch. Length: up to* **4 miles/6.5km**; *Height Climbed: negligible.*

The tidal basin of Loch Fleet is a fine place for bird watching. To reach it, follow the minor road which heads south from the A9 from near Golspie Station. The road passes the golf club then continues.

A) After a little over a mile the road reaches the car park for Balblair Wood. Cross the road and go through a gate on the far side. A map here shows the route, which is waymarked with red posts.

Follow the forest track, through pleasant pine woodland. At a junction of tracks, look for a smaller path (red) heading off to the left to reach the hide. Enjoy the view over the bay from here, then retrace your steps to return to the road.

B) Continue down the road to the car park just before Littleferry. This was once the northern end of a short (if dangerous) ferry crossing, and there are a number of points of interest. In addition to the pier, you can see the ferryman's house and an old ice house associated with the salmon fishery.

From the car park, take one of the paths leading out towards the coast. There are multiple paths leading through the undulating sandy grassland. At some point you may wish to get down to the shore, but if the tide is high it will be easier to follow the paths behind the dunes.

As the coast curves north the grassy area narrows, with a conifer plantation coming in from your left. Continue north for as far as you wish. It is possible to go all the way to Golspie, but for this walk double back before the Kart Track and return either along your original route or further inland, on the edge of the trees.